# THE NEW ESSENES

By
Sophie Edwards

Ashton House Publishing
Ashton House
High Street
Ongar
Essex CM5 9AA
United Kingdom

THIRD EDITION
ISBN: 978-0-9571301-1-1

The views expressed in this book on the subject of Christ are those of the author.

# ACKNOWLEDGEMENTS

For permission to use copyrighted material, grateful acknowledgment is made to:

The International Biogenic Society and C. W. Daniel Co. for quotations from "The Gospel of the Essenes" by Edmond Bordeaux Szekely.

Acknowledgement is also made for the quotation of T. E. Brown's poem "Indwelling."

I wish to thank all who have provided encouragement along the way and the Essene Network International for making this 3rd edition possible.

# PREFACE

The first two editions of my little book, "The New Essenes" were published in the early 1980s. Since then Dead Sea Scroll research has progressed. At times there has been considerable confusion and debate in the academic world, but majority view still considers that the Scrolls were hidden, probably even produced, by the Essenes. Material which long remained unpublished is now available to the wider public. The plan to re-print the booklet is timely as our knowledge and understanding of the Essenes has widened.

Many questions still remain unanswered about this enigmatic group. Like most other teachers of the Ancient Wisdom the Essenes passed on their carefully guarded knowledge by word of mouth or using code understood by initiates only. Much that was secret in earlier times is now widely available. This brings with it power which can be used for good or become destructive if used wrongly.

It is my hope that this little introductory booklet will be helpful for those who wish to look deeper into the message from the Scrolls. Drawing on energies, whatever name we wish to use, can be a light on the way forward. The practice of daily meditations can open many doors to inspiration and knowledge.

Sophie Edwards – June 2012

New Zealand

# FOREWORD

## BY
## SIR GEORGE TREVELYAN

The re-emergence of the Essene impulse would seem to be a phenomenon of our time and perhaps an important factor in the development of the New Age consciousness. By this I mean that we are not merely looking at the history of the sect of the Desert Fathers near the Dead Sea 2,000 years ago. The flow of history is made up of impulses expressing themselves through human souls and groups. The greatest and most all-inclusive of these is the Christ Impulse, that release into the human life-stream of the Divine Energy of Love and Unity. The chief characteristic of the New Age thinking in its manifold aspects is the recognition that the Universe is a vast continuum of Consciousness, creative and perpetually evolving. In our generation not only the mystics but the advanced scientists are arriving at the same concept: Spiritual research discovers the reality of an Ocean of Wisdom, and of Life and of Love. And the human soul is a *"point of light in a greater Light, a strand of loving energy in a sea of Love Divine, a spark of sacrificial fire, focused within the fiery Will of God."*

We must grasp this concept of the Ancient Wisdom as the Divine Source from which inspiration and guidance has worked into human evolution. This esoteric wisdom has flowed through history, manifesting in each age in a form suitable for the evolving Consciousness of the time. That which has been taught through initiation in the Mystery Temples of Antiquity rises again in the Knights Templar, the Gnostics and Cathars, the Rosicrucian teachings and the Freemasons. Often it was repressed as heresy, at times with great cruelty, for it is a perpetual challenge to rigid orthodoxy of every sort (Church, politics, science, medicine, psychology). It re-emerges powerfully in our century with the wide movement for spiritual awakening which rejects materialistic reductionism. The reality of the spiritual worlds is re-discovered. Mother earth is realized again as a living creature, an organism of which mankind is integrally part. With this knowledge we must admit to the appalling things we have done to the Earth through failure in our stewardship. Our very survival as a race now turns on a change of lifestyle and of thinking. Metanoia – *"Except ye change your thinking (mistranslated as 'repent') ye shall all likewise perish."*

The teachings and lifestyle of the Essenes were a very pure and positive expression of the Ageless Wisdom. The Essene movement has re-appeared in our generation. We are here concerned with the inspiration of Dr. Edmond Bordeaux Szekely whose translations and interpretations of the Dead Sea Scrolls and other Essene writings give a vivid and fresh understanding of the significance of this remarkable Brotherhood. Szekely's re-statement of their doctrines and teachings seems profoundly relevant to our own time. This is no narrow dogma held by men long dead. It is a living expression of eternal truths and of a lifestyle which already shows itself in many aspects of the New Age movement and awakening. Doubtless many souls who then went through the disciplines of their Rule and Lifestyle have re-incarnated again. Doubtless Szekely himself was a leading Essene teacher and has tapped the sources of his own knowledge. This is how Impulses work and flow through history. It appears that the Essene movements protected and guarded the nascent Christ Impulse and that Jesus himself was a leading initiate and believer. In our age of the Second Coming is it not likely that this group will re-emerge to continue the work? The New Age movement shows itself in the forming of innumerable groups, very varied in their nature but each concerned with an aspect of the Wholeness vision - not someone's plan for an improved society, but a tapping of springs of life and vision, bringing spirit right down into everyday life.

The Essene world-view and lifestyle may help many nowadays to understand what it is that they are really doing. Szekely's centre was in San Diego, then moved to Costa Rica. He passed on in 1979, but his work goes on through his many vivid and admirable books. He had expressed the hope that the movement would spread in Britain. It is important that it is presented afresh in our own idiom by books, Centres for Essene Lifestyle, seminars and conferences.

Therefore we welcome Sophie Edwards' book: "The New Essenes." This is a fresh and delightful statement, serving as an admirable introduction to the significance of the Essenes for our life and times. The vision will, for many, heighten the sense of meaning and purpose in what they are doing, for the Essene teachings appear to equate with the very best of our Natural Therapy and of Transpersonal Psychology, and also the Holistic Vision, which recognises the spiritual nature of man and the universe.

Szekely's *"Gospel of the Essenes"* contains translations of the Dead Sea Scrolls in a biblical and poetical form. *"The Teaching of the Essenes, from Enoch to the Dead Sea Scrolls"* is an essential commentary on the larger book. C.W.Daniel's were the publishers of the English edition of these two books. Everyone who has serious interest in this theme should read and possess this small but invaluable book. Our hope is that the New Essenes will take their place in the birth of the New Age, not by dogma, but by a broadening of understanding.

# CONTENTS

# CHAPTER 1

# BEGINNING OF A VENTURE

I had long been interested in history and the tantalising, hidden glimpses of ancient cultures held a special fascination. Information on the Essenes was difficult to find until I came across The Gospel of Essenes by Edmond Bordeaux Szekely who brought to light the hidden treasure trove of ancient teachings in a manner suitable for our age.

When the decision to hold courses on various aspects of spiritual education was taken I found I had to put my thoughts on paper to clarify them. This book contains some of the notes. The impulse to arrange such courses came in an unmistakably clear command after a meditation at a Wrekin Trust conference. I am not one of those people who hear voices or see messages flashed across walls! But the still, small voice managed to make itself heard nevertheless: I simply knew I had to hold the first residential course at our Devon home to study the beautiful poetic texts which had so captivated me.

Once the decision had been made, everything fell into shape like the last pieces of a jigsaw puzzle. Lecturers offered to help, publicity was taken care of, friends and relations were equally enthusiastic. The Higher Self, or Inner Teacher or Guide or whoever had prompted me was certainly working overtime.

As the date came nearer I started to listen for the telephone and wait for the post with an almost forgotten sense of excitement – only to find that there were no definite bookings. Then, just when I said,

"All right if this is what I am supposed to do: simply prepare everything regardless of results," the requests and bookings started coming in fast. My prayer list was fairly long and quite specific. I would like a full house but not more than twenty four at the course. We had exactly that number! Help was needed in the garden too: the rain came at the right time and just the right amount. There were two other problems: noise of traffic and neighbouring dogs. "Please let them be quiet during our noon meditation." The woodpecker made the only background noise. Every item on the list was taken care of. *"Whatsoever ye ask in prayer believing…."*

I am using my notes and diaries kept just before the course and from these I see a quite remarkable chain of events. A few weeks before the big day there came a strange testing of our determination in the form of repeated minor and not so minor accidents and setbacks. This was getting beyond a joke, I thought to myself as I sat dabbing the blood off my big toe. I had dropped a sharp tool and was sitting on the ground, nursing my foot. I had a little conversation with someone unseen, unspecified, which went something like this: "I don't know who or what you are or why you are causing me these problems. If your intention is to make me give up this plan you might as well save yourself the trouble as I am carrying on whatever happens!" There was no answer but the incidents stopped from that day on.

On Friday morning, with still plenty of preparations to do and little time left, our aged cat excelled itself and caught a young rabbit and brought it indoors. The unfortunate creature must have leapt around before it died, seemingly of fright, in the china store. The same morning a robin knocked itself dead between the sash windows. Later the cat, usually so lethargic, came in with a fledgling tree-creeper. This one we managed to save, and the joy of watching it take off made up for the loss of time spent rescuing it.

Shortly before the guests were due to arrive I thought of putting flowers in the bedrooms as a special note of welcome. It soon became obvious that each room had been used by small feathered visitors. And why a warbler should want to spend the day among the bookshelves I still have not discovered, but there it was, perched high viewing the scene. Incidentally, the swallows are raising their third brood in the toolshed after discarding a half-built nest in the garage. The site was on an empty plastic container hanging on a nail from a beam! It is the first time in sixteen years that these, my favourite birds, have chosen to live with us. Even the birds seem interested in our new venture.

*"The swallows joined us that year."*

# CHAPTER 2

# INTRODUCTION TO THE ESSENES

In 1947 a Bedouin shepherd boy found ancient manuscripts in the Judean Desert. Written in Hebrew and Aramaic the Dead Sea Scrolls, as they came to be called, were from a period which saw the beginnings of Judaism as we know it today and Christianity. The scrolls and the thousands of fragments contained the oldest extant Biblical texts and had remained free of later alterations or censorship by remaining hidden in the caves for over 2000 years. The news was heralded as the greatest manuscript discovery of the age. Some time later, when archaeology disclosed evidence at the nearby ruins at Qumran, the connection between the scrolls and the Essenes came to be generally acknowledged. Who were the Essenes and what do we know of their history?

The first indication of the formation of such a group was a period of time in Jewish history when foreign political and cultural influence caused much anxiety among pious Jews who feared the pollution and loss of sacred religious traditions. 150 BC to 140 BC is considered the date of the beginnings of the sect, but the initial period could have been several decades earlier. Unable to halt ungodly practices and revolted by the corruption of the office of the High Priest a small group followed their leader into the desert, breaking away from the religious authorities of the Jerusalem Temple. Theirs was to be 'The New Covenant' and, as the only true priests of Israel, they were to be the guardians of the Mosaic Law and all ancient traditions. In the desert they would prepare for the imminent end times and the Messianic age to follow. They are referred to as the Essenes, one of three Jewish sects mentioned by contemporary writers.

The Community Rule showed that the hierarchy at Qumran was strict and formal with the priests coming first in precedence. Rules make sure the Mosaic Law is observed in every detail, members expected to follow the regulations for a well ordered holy life at all times. Entry to this exclusive community was carefully controlled. On attaining full membership all personal property was surrendered for communal use. Not all Essenes were part of this ascetic group where the entire establishment was devoted exclusively to religion. The numbers of the Community were reported to have been 4,000 with many Essenes living ordinary lives in towns and villages. These members were not required to give up their property or remain celibate. They followed the same high ideals of the brotherhood, remained in touch, supporting each other and the central group whenever the need arose. Until the discovery of the Dead Sea Scrolls, the main source of information came from the writings of three 1st century authors: Josephus the Jewish historian, Philo of Alexandria and Pliny the Elder. It was Pliny the Elder who, as a Roman geographer and traveler, described the Essenes as a group living on the west shore of the Dead Sea.

All three authors write about the Essenes in glowing terms. Their communal lifestyle is seen as unique and particularly praiseworthy. Their dedication was to the highest ideals. Their simple lifestyle, their loving support of one another and their well ordered, creative work was admired. Josephus, having studied among the Essenes, is able to write in considerable detail about their daily practices, modes of dress, communal meals, in addition to outlining their beliefs and philosophies. He mentions their amazing ability to remain calm under extremely trying conditions. Their longevity, which he attributes to their frugal lifestyle, is amazing as is their knowledge as healers and ability to see into the future. Members must have had thorough knowledge of water conservation methods and farming practices to be able to grow food and survive in near desert conditions. The community at Qumran was exclusively male, which made later writers refer to them as a monastic establishment. The reason for celibacy of the Qumran members was that they regarded themselves as priests on permanent duty – because of the imminent end times – and as such had to observe sexual abstinence. Children placed in their care received education and careful tuition.

Josephus gives us much detailed information, but he misses out a whole lot of things which were crucial to the Essenes. We need to understand why certain important subjects are only mentioned fleetingly. As a historian, Josephus writes for a Roman/Greek audience and so there is little or no mention about the great final battle between good and evil and the victory over Satan and his ally the Kittim; code name for the Roman oppressor. Writing for a largely Roman audience it was more prudent to present the Essenes as a peaceful, loving group whose days were spent in prayer and good works. By studying the newly available manuscripts, including the highly important Rules in addition to all other available material, we can get a more realistic picture of the Essenes.

Philo the Alexandrian/Jewish philosopher gives us much information about the Essenes. Philo's fascination for interpreting Jewish Law using Greek philosophical thought has had considerable influence on the way Essene teaching was seen by later writers. His description of the Therapeautae, the contemplative Essenes, show that this group was living at the shores of Lake Mareotis near Alexandria. Philo was at home in both Jewish and Greek philosophy which he attempted to fuse and harmonise. He saw allegory as a key to understanding the mystical hidden message in the Bible and maintained that Mosaic Law was not inconsistent with the Natural Law which governs the universe. His writing, based on extensive knowledge of Jewish and Greek philosophy, had considerable influence on Medieval Christian theology as well as inspiring later authors.

It is important to remember that as guardians of the ancient priestly traditions the innermost knowledge was only disclosed to initiates. We are fortunate to have access to much inside information about the Essenes. Their beliefs, organisation and practices can now be better understood through the Scrolls which we can study in addition to the writings of contemporary authors. For further reading I would strongly recommend "The Complete Dead Scrolls in English" by Geza Vermes.

There appears no sign of the Essenes after the destruction of Qumran by the Roman army in AD 68. Much about the Essenes still remains a mystery. What we do know is that since the discovery of the Scrolls there is now far more known about Jewish history during the period between 200 BC and 70 AD. This has given us new information about the background from which Christianity emerged. Practices, rituals and even words attributed to Jesus, once thought to be unique, were found in the manuscripts associated with Qumran and the Essenes. When reading passages from the New Testament and the Scrolls, one cannot fail to notice the similarities in the way both expect the end times to be near. This emphasis is also found in the message of Jesus who speaks of the kingdom soon to come. Much regarding the Essenes and the early Church forms the subject of ongoing discussion and speculation, including John the Baptist and Jesus whose person is seen in as many forms as the many theories that abound. It was said of the Essenes that "they walked with the angels." We need to tread the same path, and see how study and meditation leads to new insight.

The 'Tree of Life' will be the subject of the next chapter. It is an ancient symbol, found in many cultures and interpreted in many ways, through the ages.

# CHAPTER 3

# THE ANCIENT WISDOM TEACHING FOR OUR TIME

# THE ONE LAW AND THE TREE OF LIFE

*"Your Father is the Cosmos. Your Mother is Nature.*
*Your brothers are your fellowmen.*
*Live in harmony with the laws and forces of the universe,*
*and nature and your own being.*
*Preserve (love) yourself,*
*Learn the natural and cosmic laws,*
*Live in peace with yourself, with humanity,*
*with nature and the universe.*
*Live in creative love with and for your fellowmen*
*that they may live for you.*
*Peace be with you."*

The words of Banus the master to his pupil Josephus. The time: almost two thousand years ago. The place: somewhere in the desert in the Middle East. As I read these words the birds sing in the mist of a rainy autumn evening. The distant rumble of traffic reminds me of the twentieth century. Outwardly our world differs from that of the Essenes but their teaching is as valid today as it was then: *"Come ye, and let us walk in the light of the Law."* Call it God, or the Lord or the Law. It matters little what word you use as long as you are at peace with it.

# THE TREE OF LIFE.

Cultures and religions used symbols since time immemorial. It was a powerful way to convey messages and it could be used to pass on information which was meant for initiates only.

The Tree of Life was used widely and in many different forms. Corresponding to the tree and its branches we have teachings from the East of the 7 chakras through which cosmic energy or prana enters the body. Nordic mythology speaks of the sacred tree Ygdrasil and many more examples could be quoted. The Tree of Knowledge appears in legends from ancient Babylonia symbolising the quest for immortality.

Jewish mystical tradition goes back to Moses and earlier. The Cosmic Tree of Life is presented as a Map for the contemplative journey to the Divine. The Tree is used as an aid in many ancient Jewish meditating techniques with the mystical traveler ascending to Worlds or Heavenly Realms. Angels were seen as the forces of the universe, often called messengers from on high. There is now a renewed longing for co-operation with nature in all its forms. New ways are being discovered since the phenomenal growth of the Findhorn garden appeared to be due to communication with Devas - nature spirits.

According to tradition Moses received the Holy Law on Mt. Sinai. Whichever way we read this passage in the Bible we are aware that it signifies a momentous event in evolution of consciousness. The One Law which is above all other laws is to be entrusted to Moses together with secrets which could be of untold benefit for humankind.

We know the end: people were unprepared, the tablets got broken, the secret teaching remained hidden for centuries. Few written records were available because instruction was "from mouth to ear" and referred to by various names, often in code. Increased demand for more information and access to better translation and new discoveries has lifted the veil of secrecy. The result has been a renewed interest not just in Eastern mysticisms but in Western mystical teaching with its roots in the Kabbalah. The discovery of the Scrolls has led to an upsurge of interest in the hidden teaching of the Essenes. Based on wide knowledge of ancient cultures, using intuition and inspired interpretation, Edmond Szekely's method is followed here.

The Angels (forces or energies) of the universe are represented by the branches and the roots of the tree. Heavenly Father, Eternal Life, Creative Work, Peace, Power Love and Wisdom are the seven unseen heavenly cosmic forces. The roots symbolise the Earthly Mother, Earth, Life trees (strength), Joy, Sun, Water, and Air. Illustration showed the person sitting at the base of the tree: with the lower chakras drawing energy from the earthly forces and the chakras situated higher in the body close to the energy from worlds above.

As outlined by contemporary reports the meditation schedule started at dawn focusing on the sun and the earthly forces. At the end of the day the Angels were invoked to guide thoughts heavenward during sleep. The three periods of regular prayer and contemplation, certain breathing practices, frugal habits and the well ordered lifestyle are mentioned by Josephus. This is a pattern we can follow as we consciously co-operate with creative forces. The popularity and effectiveness of Bio-Dynamic farming which is based on co-operation with natural forces  of  Nature cannot be denied. Having got into the habit of filling our mind with thoughts which are health-giving the next step is to learn how to direct these currents of energy by encouraging  positive thoughts.

It has been said that many people showing such interest in the Essenes today could have been members of the Brotherhood in a previous lifetime on earth. Whatever one's views on reincarnation may be one thing is certain: we have it in our power to create a better world, starting with our own health by using our thoughts creatively.

A single phrase came into my consciousness most recently: *"Be in this world, yet not of it."* There are those who can set themselves apart and live as a group where life can be fashioned on more spiritual concepts. Many of us would gladly do this but must realise that we are where we are for a very special purpose. We can and must contribute to preparing the way by creating in our own surroundings a situation, an atmosphere into which Christ can be re-born in Spirit. We can and should study and follow teachings which lift our awareness from self-consciousness to God-consciousness. In this way we help to create a community into which the teachers of the new age can be born.

# CHAPTER 4

# THE SEVENFOLD PEACE

Each of the Noon Contemplations focuses on one aspect of the Sevenfold Peace.

Peace with the Kingdom of the Heavenly Father
Peace with the Kingdom of the Earthly Mother
Peace with Culture
Peace with Humanity
Peace with the Family
Peace with the Mind
Peace with the Body

We do well to stop our activities even for a few minutes at midday. It can be a magic moment; a lull in the rush and bustle. Spend a few minutes away from noise, becoming centred, finding that source within us which creates harmony. If we can make this period a 10-15 minute break from mundane thoughts and activities all the better but even a few minutes are beneficial. Such practice helps us to get our priorities right and by stilling our minds we replenish our depleted stocks of energy. Our thoughts leave the trivial for a few minutes and focus on the highest: Peace with the Creative Source, the Heavenly Father. More and more people are becoming conscious of the need to live in harmony with all creatures rather than depleting and destroying ruthlessly what Mother Earth has provided. As we contemplate and give thanks for the gifts of our earthly Mother our attitude to food changes. Kirlian photography shows that cooking with love alters the food we prepare, giving it some indefinable, vital quality. Pausing for a few minutes at midday we examine our relationships, with the family, friends, our workmates, and neighbours. We refuse to become submerged in the tide of negative information knowing that there is an ocean of good around us. Peace with culture is not limited to an occasional visit to an art exhibition or library, but should become a regular habit which looks for and delights in all the beauty that we as human beings have created. True peace with body and mind can only be achieved if we realise that we are spiritual beings. Body, mind and spirit must be in harmony. One way of achieving this is by eating wholefoods and "live" foods: sprouting legumes and wholegrains. Nuts, seeds and the small growing shoots of vegetables are the life-generating "Biogenic" foods which should form 25% of our daily diet. They can be easily and cheaply obtained at home all the year round. Fresh raw foods should be taken daily, forming as much as 50% of our diet, the rest to be made up of cooked wholefoods. Unfortunately many people in the West live almost wholly on denatured refined, processed convenience foods which can actually harm our health. The International Biogenic Society classified these as Biocidic (pronounced as in genocide) foods and recommends that they be avoided altogether. And above all remember meal times should be relaxed, happy occasions. Tension, angry thoughts and hate can poison the body.

All teachers of the Ancient Wisdom knew that thoughts were powerful tools. The way in which our thoughts affect our health has become widely recognized. Wholistic healing is a concept which is being re-discovered in our age as it is seen how tension, angry thoughts and hate can poison the body. The power of positive thought and visualisation is used in many ways: healing, education, and training. It is a tool which can help us to reach our potential. Remember that we can actively co-operate in saving the world by sending out thoughts of love and healing. Never underestimate the power of creative energy of thought but use it to bring peace, harmony and health.

CHAPTER 5

# BE STILL – KNOW I AM GOD

Through the practice of meditation we train our bodies to relax and our minds to be calm. We create a centre of stillness into which inspiration can enter, and through which our whole being can begin to function more efficiently. Our mind is like Charing Cross Station during the rush hour: noisy and crowded. To make matters worse many of our thoughts chasing each other are useless, trivial or even harmful thoughts which waste and drain our energies. Meditation is a form of mental spring-cleaning, of uncluttering. It can give a new dimension to our lives. As we reach out to the highest within ourselves, the God-like part in us can, in time, transform our whole being. The loving joyful outlook extends to those around us in an ever widening circle.

There are many methods of meditation, but most have certain things in common. First you find a quiet place where you can come to each day at a certain time. Regularity is important as you are training the subconscious which is a creature of habit. It is possible to meditate in any comfortable position but sitting upright with the spine straight helps to maintain alertness. Preparation for meditation is very important. It is difficult to relax completely if you think you might be interrupted at any time during your 'quiet' half hour. Twenty minutes morning and evening with a short period at midday would be ideal, but even a few minutes twice or three times a day helps. It is better not to choose a time directly after a meal. Another thing to remember is that it is difficult to meditate if you are very tired mentally or physically. In such a case it would be better to have a period of deep relaxation followed by a short sleep before trying to sit in meditation.

It is important for the body to be totally relaxed during meditation. This is why we are told to sit in a position in which we can remain comfortable without moving during the period of meditation. Give your body special attention thinking of each part in turn, tell it to relax, to let go of all tension. Or you can tighten each set of muscles in turn and then consciously relax them. Pay special attention to the tension areas of shoulders, neck and face. Some methods advocate certain exercises before sitting down to meditate. Almost all advise you to take a few deep breaths and then to let the breath come easily, regularly. Up to now we have dealt with the preparations only – but in it lies half the success.

Concentration is a skill essential to meditation and for this reason we are sometimes told to fix the attention on a candle or a flower for a certain length of time, then close the eyes and visualize the image as long as it can be held. Mindfulness of breathing is another method. In this the breath is watched as it goes in.... and out regularly. The attention is fixed on the breathing. With each in-breath you can silently say to yourself the word: Love. You are drawing in the cosmic energy of love. With each out-breath you are consciously sending out life-giving energy of Love. The attention is fixed on the breath which is never forced, just smooth and relaxed.

As you create a fully relaxed condition in your body so your mind becomes calmer. If thoughts intrude, don't get cross or agitated but just gently tell them to go away, to be dealt with later. This emptying of the mind, keeping in neutral gear, so to speak, is important and can be quite difficult. The use of short affirmations, or images, and sounds, can be very helpful. Meditate just for a short while each day at first. Never force the issue, just exercise gentle self-discipline. Good preparation and regular practice will bring results in time.

Yoga and Tai-Chi are meditative exercises. In remedial meditation visualisation is used to correct disharmony in the system and improve the function of the part of the body which needs healing. Creative imagination guided by another person, or done alone, is also used. Among other advantages, it helps to develop the subtle senses through which we can become more sensitive, more able to reach a state of inner quietness which opens us to inspiration and intuition. Methods of teaching which are using relaxation and meditation as an approach to learning have shown remarkable, even astounding, success rates.

Sound can play an important part and the use of a mantra is widespread, especially in the East, though we must not forget that the West has used this form in prayers such as the Litany. A mantra is a word for a short sentence which is repeated until it imprints itself on the subconscious and then returns to the conscious mind unbidden together with the response originally associated with it. Used correctly and with the right intent, it is a most effective and efficient way of concentrating the mind. But it is very important to make sure that you know what the mind is concentrating on and it was for this reason that in the past a name of God, or a quality of an aspect of God, was used and not just a meaningless word. A sound repeated in this fashion creates its own powerful vibratory energy which can affect the user at all levels. It is like a boat, which is set to steer itself. This is why the choice of the boat, the prayerful thought and the right intention is all important.

Whichever method we adopt, the aim is to create an inner peace or stillness, a clean empty temple of the mind into which inspiration can enter. T.E. Brown's poem describes it beautifully:

*"If thou could'st empty all thyself of self*
*Like to a shell dishabited*
*Then might He find thee on an ocean shelf*
*And say 'This is not dead'*
*And fill thee with Himself instead.*

*But thou art so replete with very thou*
*And hast such shrewd activity*
*That when He comes He'll say: 'It is enow*
*Unto itself – 'twere better let it be:*
*It is so small and full*
*And has no need of me."*

Sir George liked to add a third verse which he wrote himself:

*"So will I empty all myself of self*
*Like to a shell dishabited*
*Then will He find me on an ocean shelf*
*And say 'This is not dead'*
*And fill me with Himself instead."*

To use the words of Sir George Trevelyan in his book "The Vision of the Aquarian Age" - *"Our materialistic civilisation is largely concerned with looking outward. Meditation balances this tendency by turning us inwards and so through into realms of extended awareness."*

Meditation is silent prayer – it is a time when we quieten ourselves to hear the still, small voice. *"Be still, know I am God."*

A word on the question of protection. This is a term I heard frequently when first starting to meditate. Many people seemed very concerned with it, a fact which I found somewhat puzzling. I could see the necessity of bringing the consciousness back slowly from the heightened sensitivity reached during meditation – rather like a diver has to take time to surface. I felt more comfortable if I allowed my mind to make the adjustment from the inner stillness to the everyday hustle and bustle. But protection? Then I heard an explanation which clarified the question for me. Put in a few words, the answer was this: your body is surrounded by a force field or barrier which acts as a filter and shields you against all sorts of incoming forces like germs, certain rays, harmful vibrations from negative thought forms, etc. This barrier or auric field, as it is sometimes called, is kept intact and healthy the same way as the rest of your body, that is by right food, right thoughts and feelings and so on. Through various methods this barrier is thinned or parted during meditation so that the forces or energies you wish to contact may have access to your whole being for healing yourself or to channel healing through you. In meditation we consciously 'open' and if we are going to open ourselves to outside influences we had better make sure they are the right ones! This is why ancient teachers all over the world used a sacred name as a mantra or followed some other form of ritual practice before and after meditation. Ultimately the only real protection is the pure intention. Meditation for selfish reasons, either to gain power or satisfy idle curiosity or even search for spiritual knowledge for the sake of knowing more is not the right intention. In meditation we ask for guidance for all problems and learn to 'listen' to the Inner Teacher, the High Self, the Christ within. Such meditation is more than just stress release. It is dynamic and can change our whole life. We are in touch with tremendously powerful influences while meditating. In addition to the right intention it is important to see ourselves as channels through which these healing energies can flow. Close your meditation with a heartfelt Thank You and remember the old Indian saying: "All evil vanishes from life for him who has the sun shining in his heart." Imagine the warmth and the life-giving powers of the sun – and enfold yourself in the protective cloak of Love, or you may like to visualize yourself surrounded by light.

# CHAPTER 6

# DAILY MEDITATION GUIDE

Certain times of the day have been considered of special significance in many cultures. Great importance was attached to greeting the new day and preparing for night time and the period of sleep. Noon was also regarded as special. Body and mind need the short rest at mid day. In some parts of the world even nature seems to remain silent for a little while at noon. It is not difficult to imagine the community at Qumran: the magic moment of sunrise, light and shade over the desert landscape at noon and the silence of the myriad stars at night.

These times were set aside for contemplation and communion with the forces of the Universe. On waking and immediately before sleep, the mind is in a borderland of consciousness. The subconscious is very receptive to ideas at this time. A thought held strongly before the mind becomes involved with daily problems will imprint itself on the subconscious in the way a mantra does. Example: Tuesday morning, the first thought on waking is *"Angel of Joy....give beauty to all things."* It is easy to see how, with time and correct practice, this can give a new dimension to life. The evening was considered the beginning of the day. It is during sleep that the preparation for the following twenty four hours begins. It is not just a period of rest for the body but a time when we enter a very important learning process during which we are in touch with unseen higher forces. That is why we are told to hold the thought we meditated upon in the evening and not to lose it through chatter and distracting activities. We go into sleep with the thought of this uplifting, inspiring, strengthening, beneficial force around us. That opens us to inspirations. *"Sleep on it"* is a saying of great ancient wisdom. This is why sudden inspirations often come in the morning on waking, giving the solution which eluded our minds the day before.

*"For by day we shall commune with the Angels of the Earthly Mother. By night we shall commune with the Angels of the Heavenly Father;*

*And when the sun reacheth the zenith at noontide, we shall stand silent before the Sevenfold Peace; and no evil shall befall us."*

## Friday Evening *"The Heavenly Father and I are One"*

In keeping with Jewish custom, the week started on Friday evening when the Essenes welcomed the Sabbath with prayer. This is the point at which we contemplate the cosmic currents, the final Union with the Cosmic Ocean of Divinity. The ultimate goal where there is no separation between the soul and God.

*"If I take the wings of the morning*
*And dwell in the uttermost parts of the sea,*
*Even there shall thy hand lead me,*
*And thy right hand shall hold me."*

Sitting quietly in front of the fire there is no sound. These moments when the precious stillness is complete are rare. Only the flames whisper. Outside night has fallen. There is a song without words. *"Night unto night announces the Knowledge."* I hear the clock striking in the Church tower, but time has stopped: it is Eternal Now.

*"Before the mountains were brought forth, or ever thou hadst formed the Earth; even from Everlasting to Everlasting Thou art God. And who maketh the plants? Who to the wind hath yoked the storm-clouds? The*

*swift and even the fleetest? Who, oh Great Creator is the fountain of*
*Eternal Life within our souls?"*

The turning point in life comes when we realise that we are never alone. We each have a High Self, the divine within. Hold this thought in your heart in the quiet time before the day is over.

## Saturday Morning
Earthly Mother
Digestive Organs
Food
Nutrition

*"The Earthly Mother and I are one. She gives the food of life to*
*my whole body."*

With your subtler senses awakened, walk into a garden full of fruit and vegetables. Smell the fragrance of the fresh growth and pick some of the fruit. Look at the colours, feel the texture and the weight. Gather some vegetables and take delight in the crisp fresh green leaves of a lettuce – the sun-ripened warmth of a tomato. Look towards the fields and see the green grass. Hear the wind and see it rippling the ripe corn. Now focus your attention on this thought: the energies of Mother Earth are like currents flowing around you, through you, into you. Welcome these forces, open yourself to them in consciousness. Encourage them throughout the day by eating those foods which are life-giving. Our bodies are formed out of the elements of the Earthly Mother. We draw strength from her. Acknowledge this help and repay it with gratitude: look after and cherish all living things around you. If you do not have access to a garden you may like to place before you a bowl of fruit of some flowers.

*"Honour thy Earthly Mother, that thy days may be long upon the land. Thy Earthly Mother is in thee, and thou in her. She bore thee; she giveth thee life. It was she who gaveth thee thy body, and to her shall thou one day give it back again......The blood that runs in us is born of the blood of our Earthly Mother. Her blood falls from the clouds, leaps up from the womb of the earth, babbles in the brooks of the mountains, flows wide in the rivers of the plains, sleeps in the lakes, rages mightily in the tempestuous seas. The air which we breathe is born of the breath of the Earthly Mother. Her breath is azure in the heights of the heavens, soughs in the tops of the mountains, whispers in the leaves of the forest, billows over the cornfields, slumbers in the deep valleys and burns hot in the desert. The hardness of our bones is born of the bones of our Earthly Mother, of the rocks and the stones. They stand naked to the heavens on the tops of the mountains. They are as giants that lie sleeping on the side of the mountains, as idols set in the desert, and re hidden in the deepness of the earth. The tenderness of our flesh is born of the flesh of our Earthly Mother whose flesh waxeth yellow and red in the fruits of the trees, and nurtures us in the furrows of the fields. The light of our eyes, the hearing of our ears, both are born of the colours and sounds of our Earthly Mother and from her did the Son of Man receive her whole body even as the newborn babe is born of the womb of the Earthly Mother."*

Remain in silence for a while letting the echo of these words resonate in you.

Now send out healing loving thoughts to all especially to those who work with Mother Earth. Also those engaged in research, and those preparing food. *"From the point of light within the mind of God, let light stream forth into the minds of men."* Send out this light so that they understand the importance of seeing Mother Earth as a living being to be cherished, and treated with loving respect.

*"Let light and love and power restore the plan on Earth."*

**Saturday Noon** Peace with the Kingdom of the Heavenly Father

*"Our Father, who art in Heaven, send to all your Angel of Peace: to your*
*Kingdom, our Heavenly Father, your Angel of Eternal Life."*

This is the peace which contains all other aspects of peace, the peace of God which passeth all understanding. There is deep yearning for such inner peace in all of us.

*"Have ye not known? Have ye not heard?*
*Hath it not been told thee from the beginning?*
*Lift up thine eyes on high, and behold the Holy Law*
*Which was established before the eternal,*
*Sovereign and luminous space,*
*Which hath created the foundations of the earth,*
*Which is the first and the last,*
*Which liveth in the hearts of the Children of Light.*
*For the Law is great,*
*As the Heavenly Father is great above his Angels:*
*It is He who giveth us the Law, and He is the Law."*

The Law is everywhere It is the ultimate Truth behind all that happened in the Universe. It is a natural law, not a manmade law. It is universal and is not confined to any creed or theology. Names such as Heavenly Father, or Lord, or God are outer garments of a concept that cannot be put into words. Years ago a sentence flashed into my mind: *"There will be no peace until you are one with God."* I wondered what this meant, especially as it came at a quiet and happy period in my life. Then, a few years later, another sentence, *"You will never be alone – Christ is always with you."* This too happened when I was in a very contented frame of mind – not thinking of anything more complicated than why there were no blackberries on that particular side of the hedge! We must regard ourselves as part of the universe, as part of the whole. Each of us is a powerhouse of energy because of the eternal, indestructible divine spark within. Reach out to the Higher Self, to the Inner Teacher; to the Christ who gives *"the peace of your Earthly Mother to your body, and the peace of the Heavenly Father to your spirit. And let the peace of both reign among the Sons of Man."*

**Saturday Evening**    The Angel of Eternal Life
                                     Planets
                                     Overcoming Gravity


*"Angel of Eternal Life descend upon me and give eternal life*
*to my spirit"*


*Let me become aware that my spirit is eternal. Let me accept and fully believe that life is never-ending, because death is just a transformation from one state to another and not the end. Our goal is to become one with Life Eternal. Lift your head high, look up and be proud of your inheritance. The attributes of God: Limitless Power, absolute Harmony, Eternal duration.*
  *"While we are children we will see the stars,*
  *But not the hand which scatters them*
  *Through the sky as the farmer scatters his seed;*
  *Only through the Communions*
  *With the Angels of the Heavenly Father,*
  *Will we learn to see the unseen,*
  *To hear that which cannot be heard,*
  *And to speak the unspoken word."*

As humans we are considered to have free will. Even if limited by circumstances, we do have some freedom of choice. During the course of our evolution we were given the experience of learning to know matter. We have delved deeply into it, studied it, become fascinated with it and even misused it. The Divine energy of love and unity is the liberating power. We must remember that we are of the spirit. We must create preconditions in our lives in which the spirit in us can move freely. Like the gardener we must prepare the ground first before sowing the seed. Clear the weeds and feed the soil; get our priorities right. Simplify our lives, de-clutter and then feed body, mind and spirit.

In ancient days mystery schools taught secret methods by which higher powers could be contacted and used to help mankind. Today much of this knowledge is no longer secret – science and recent discoveries are throwing open the doors which were locked for centuries: our power is great. This is not just because in our time we are more ready and able to accept and understand the unseen, as we have become used to modern invention. We have tremendous powers to counteract the destructive forces. Faced with great changes in today's world, confronted with the unknown it would be all too easy to feel helpless and fearful. The greater the anxiety is at the present state of the world, the more we have to know how to react to it by reaching to the power of Christ, and lifting our thoughts above the gravity of the downward pull. All so-called black magicians know that they can only keep hold of us and further their destructive plans by spreading fear. A fearful person can be more easily led into foolish actions. It is our task to transform fear into hope. Visualize this fear as a dense cloud round the earth and go through it, into the warm light: the Christ sun. Rise into the blue skies and sunshine like an aircraft flying over the clouds.

**Sunday Morning**      Angel of Earth
Topsoil
Regeneration
New life
Generative organs

*"Angel of Earth enter my generative organs and regenerate
my whole body."*

The life force, the power of generation and regeneration is manifest through Earth. Think of the topsoil – the precious few inches covering our earth. It is here that the seeds germinate and grow to clothe the earth with grass and trees and various forms of vegetation. Destroy this 'skin' covering Mother Earth and you destroy life. Think of the deep carpet of leaves which rot down into humus. The falling leaf, its work accomplished becomes transformed in the soil to give vital nourishment to new life. Meditate on this new life from old. The old is not discarded as useless, rather it becomes a gracious ingredient to sustain the new. There is no death, only change, only a transformation from one kind of existence into another.

This life force, this all important power of creating new bodies, works in us through our organs of regeneration. It manifests in every cell creating abundant new life. The powers of procreation were regarded as sacred in ancient times. The male and female in all its aspects formed the basis of ritual and religious cults because continuation of life was considered the most important function. It is only the deviation from the pure and holy Law that has profaned the sacred. Our task is not to ignore or suppress sex but to bring to it the spiritual qualities of loving relationship and joy.

The sexual energy is a most powerful generator: its force can be used not only to create new physical life but spiritualized it can give birth to a new self, a new humanity. Empty ourselves first of all pre-conceived notions, judgments, and earthly concepts, and let the Divine fill this empty space. This is the meaning of virgin birth, a story found in so many mythologies. *"You are a member of a species that reproduces through sexual desire. Any game you play to deny the existence of this is denying the way God is manifesting in this particular form. The game is not to deny the desire but to extricate yourself from identification with it."(Ram Dass)* Our task is to bring a new understanding to these concepts – and in spite of all the dark forces swilling their dirt around, who can say that there is not the beginning of a new awareness for the quality of life and a reverence for life itself.

There is increasing awareness of ecology and conservation and kindness to animals. Communities such as Findhorn, the Centre for Alternative Technology, the Bio-Dynamic Agriculture Centres, the Friends of the Earth and many others show that today we are becoming more aware of our most precious heritage, the soil. Of course really good farmers always knew this – but they are men of few words preferring to get on with the job. *"He who sows corn, grass and fruit soweth the Law….he maketh the Law of the Creator to progress. When all the Earth shall be a garden, then shall all the bodily world become free, from old age and death, from corruption and rot, forever and forever. Mercy and truth shall meet together. Righteousness and peace shall kiss each other. Truth shall spring out of the earth and glory shall dwell in our land."*

Take this vision into your hearts and minds today. It must become a reality in our thoughts before it can come to be a reality in the material world.

### Sunday Noon   Peace with the Kingdom of the Earthly Mother

*"Our Father who art in Heaven, send to all your Angel of Peace; to the Kingdom of our Earthly Mother, your Angel of Joy"*

None of us are isolated particles of this earth. There is an inter-relationship between all things, human, animal, plant, mineral and all the unseen forces. The health of one affects the other. At some level we are all one. Unless man is at peace with his surroundings he cannot find peace and health himself. *"Thou art one with the Earthly Mother; she is in thee and thou in her.... Keep therefore her laws, for none can live long, neither be happy but he who honours his Earthly Mother and doeth her laws."*

Teach your children a reverence of growing things... There are so many ways you can help Mother Earth. Do it now, start today. Our combined action together with the thoughts of all those wanting to help will form a great force for good. It is said that in ancient Persia a father planted a fruit tree on each birthday of his son. Then when the boy reached the age of twenty one he was given the orchard which he had learnt to tend. We can encourage our children to plant things – even if it is just a little cress and mustard. *"So shall we love and care for the trees that grow in our land, so shall we keep and protect them that they may grow tall and strong – and fill the earth again with their beauty. For the trees are our brothers, and as brethren we shall guard and love them."*

The words of the ancient wisdom ring loud the warning: "To obtain the treasures of the material world, O sons of men, forego not the word of the law." It is folly to think that cruel exploitation of other living creatures can benefit us in any way. Only if we keep the great law of nature can we survive on this earth.

**Sunday Evening**     Angel of Creative Work
                       Bees
                       Creative work of man


*"Angel of Creative Work, descend upon humanity and give*
*abundance to all men."*


*"The Fifth Communion is with the Angel of Work*
*Who sings in the humming of the bee,*
*Pausing not in making of golden honey;*
*In the flute of the shepherd,*
*Who sleeps not lest his flock go astray;*
*In the song of the maiden*
*As she lays her hand on the spindle.*
*And if you think that these*
*Are not as fair in the eyes of the Lord*
*As the loftiest of prayers*
*Echoed from the highest mountain,*
*Then you do indeed err,*
*For the honest work of humble hands*
*Is a daily prayer of thanksgiving*
*And the music of the plough*
*Is a joyful song unto the Lord."*

A traveller from the East remarked on his first visit to the West: "You seem to be rushing through one job in order to get to the next one." We would do well to stop and think and review our priorities. Separate the essential from the unessential. Simplify our lives. Why am I doing this particular job? Is it really serving a useful purpose? Helping my development, my peace of mind? Is it serving the good of the community? There are quite a few daily tasks we may be able to revise if we just take time to sit down and think quietly before charging into the work to be done.

The second most helpful piece of advice for me was this rather trite sentence: *"Happiness is not doing what you like, but liking what you're doing."* Much energy is wasted in resenting a job, in wishing you were through with it. If we put our full attention and energy into the present moment and find satisfaction in doing it, the task becomes lighter.

Think of the wonderful things created by human beings. The great works of art, music and literature. The fine buildings, the beauty of some of the objects we use daily, and their usefulness. Then think of the bees at work. Visualize them collecting honey. See the bright yellow pollen on their feet as they emerge from among the petals of a flower. Hear their humming as they carry their treasure back to the hive. What single-mindedness, what order they exhibit! Look at and perhaps reconsider your values in life. Has the rush for more material goods made us miss the goal? Can we find satisfaction, peace and health again? Learn from the book of nature and apply it to our lives. *"Then shall the Kingdom of Heaven fill all the earth with glory. And the shining stars of the most high shall blaze within the hearts of the Children of Light, warm and comfort the seeking sons of men."*

## Monday Morning

Angel of Life
Trees
Vitality
Bone structure, Muscles

*"Angel of Life, enter my limbs and give strength to my whole body."*

Saying this I breathe deeply, drawing the life force and vitality into me. The force which is all around me, which makes an acorn grow into an oak tree. Thinking of the trees and forests I walk under the green domes and see the sunshine through the leaves. The many shades of green which give a sense of harmony. Consciously think of strength and vitality entering my limbs, my whole body. Summer or winter, weather does not matter as I begin to use my subtler senses and imagine myself walking in the woods.

Today it is warm, so I can actually go out to my favourite tree, a large conifer. My grandson was fascinated at the tree being called Sequoia after the great Indian chief. "The Indians talked to trees," he told me. So did many others – including presumably the Essenes. I sit down on the large stone which serves as a seat at the base of the tree, with my back resting against the trunk, watching the sun rise on this summer morning, drawing the life force and energy into me with every breath.

*"Go then towards the high growing trees*
*And before one of them which is beautiful,*
*High growing and mighty, say these words:*
*"Hail unto thee, O good living tree, made by the Creator,*
*Then shall the river of life flow between*
*You and your Brother the Tree.."*

Closing my eyes I think of the roots of this tree. The main roots and the network of tiny ones drawing nourishment from deep in the soil. With my inner ears I hear the sap rising. I open my eyes and look up into the branches and marvel at the green leaves which can change sunshine into food. Man too has an ability to draw on the energies of nature. The first step towards this is to regard food as a sacrament, with reverence. In the stillness I let the vitality of the tree flow into me, becoming one with the tree in thought and feeling. *"I speak to you through the trees of the forest. Be still. Know I am God."*

Hold this silence.

*"Seek not the law in thy scriptures for the law is life whereas the scriptures are only words."* This is not meant to belittle our great cultural heritage but to teach us to read the book of nature. During the morning Communions we learn to become more sensitive to what the Earthly Mother tells us, more receptive to the life-giving earthly forces.

*"The law is the living word of living God to living prophets for living men. In everything that is life the law is written; it is found in the grass, in the trees, in the river, in the mountains, in the birds of heaven, in the forest creatures and the fishes of the sea; but it is found chiefly in thy heart and in thy spirit."*

We become deeply aware of all the precious things of the earth, and send love and light to the whole world.

"Go then towards the high growing trees..."

## Monday Noon     Peace with Culture

*"Our Father who art in Heaven, send to all your Angel of Peace. To Our knowledge the Angel of Wisdom."*

In the morning we studied the book of nature; the noon contemplation directs our attention to the creative masterpieces of all ages and cultures.

According to the ancient schools the three ways of learning were: through intuition which was the method used by the mystics: through observation by careful study of nature's laws. The third way of gaining knowledge was by learning from our cultural heritage from the great masterpieces of art and literature.

The first is now being rediscovered and used in many 'new' ways of teaching a wide variety of subjects from creative to languages, sport and many more basic disciplines like reading. Essentially the method is to create around you and within your whole body a relaxed, tension free condition which lets all parts of your mind function equally. The method does not eliminate the need for study but simply releases tensions which could prevent the brain from functioning efficiently. For several centuries we have perfected the left side of the brain: the rational analytical part of our thinking. The right side from which comes creative imagination, intuition and inspiration was even regarded with mistrust. We are beginning to realize that both must be developed to achieve our full potential. So the scientists are discovering what the mystics have said for ages. It is only the idiom that has changed.

Let us in this noon contemplation on Peace with culture examine how we make use of the third way of learning: of gaining knowledge and wisdom through culture.

With the ease of printing a vast number of books are being published today. How many of them contain really good, nourishing food for the mind? Or how much of what we read makes us happy and joyful? If the answers to these questions are not too encouraging, then on the credit side is the fact that libraries are used by a great number of people of all ages and that through modern inventions cultural knowledge can reach those who may otherwise be cut off from it.

Let us lift our awareness to reach the Ocean of Thought from which the great writers and artists drew their inspirations. Let us make a clean, empty space in ourselves for the Universal Mind to fill with Wisdom. We do not need to sit on a mountain or meditate in the solitude of the desert. But from today, from this hour I will make an effort to unclutter my mind. Instead of harmful and useless information make room for thoughts which build peace and harmony.

## Monday Evening
Angel of Peace
Crescent Moon

*"Peace, peace, peace, Angel of Peace be always everywhere."*

This is the keyword: peace. Repeat it over and over. We all have at times fallen short of it. Don't dwell on the moments when chaos reigned. Let the peace of God which passeth all understanding surround you. Feel it stilling the turmoil.

Nature has an inbuilt ability for harmony and balance. Learn from it, follow its promptings. Too long have I resisted. Why all this rush? What really matters is to be at peace with myself and with God. Everything else will take care of itself. All is in the hands of a loving helper, provided I am willing to cooperate. Let God and let be....

*"Peace dwells in the heart of silence. Be still and know I am God."*

Visualise the moon reflected on the surface of a calm lake. Let the stillness of the night sky give stillness to my whole being. Absorb this peace, become one with it.

Now it is time to send out thoughts of peace. Your thoughts are joining the great wave of powerful thoughts of others around the world. We have been given freewill and because of this the higher powers must await our initiative. Ask for peace and visualise it.

*"In the reign of peace there is neither hunger nor thirst...Neither cold wind nor hot wind..."* Visualise the world at peace, loving and loved.

It is possible. *"Whatever you ask believing – you already have it."* This is the secret, to really believe that light and love can bring peace to all.

*"Let the plan of Love and Light work out. And may it transmute evil into good."*

*Peace, peace, peace be always everywhere.*

**Tuesday Morning**     Angel of Joy

Beauty

Harmony

*"Angel of Joy, descend upon Earth and give beauty to all beings."*

As I wake up I let my mind dwell on something beautiful like a sunrise or a colourful flower. My consciousness is returning slowly from sleep and I open the windows of the mind to let the sunshine flood in.

There are times when everything seems grey and almost unbearably depressing. I know from experience that if such thoughts are given a perch to settle then they will make themselves at home. Don't allow them to find a foothold. Get pencil and paper and write down three things on the credit side in your life. Then add two more everyday! Our whole system benefits from being open to joy and beauty of God's creation.

*"For the Lord is not worshipped with sadness nor with cries of despair. Leave off your moans and lamentations and sing unto the Lord a new song...Sing unto the Lord all the Earth....."*

The Polynesian healer priests achieved amazing cures by teaching their patients to think not of the present state of disease for which they had come to seek a cure, but to visualise their bodies as full of health and vitality. We do not deny the existence of evil, but so fill our minds with joyful positive thoughts that gradually the negative will wither away. A similar technique is used today with considerable success. Patients are trained to reconstruct their thoughts to regain health. Much energy is wasted by feelings of guilt for past deeds and by worry over the future, fretting about things which may never happen! This effort is better spent on shaping the present.

Today I will watch all my thoughts and see how I react to any news. My thoughts will be "What can I learn from this? What is this meant to teach me? How can I turn this to the best advantage?" The effect of this attitude cannot be over-estimated.

*"Let the Heavens rejoice and the Earth be glad."*

## Tuesday Noon    Peace with Humanity

*"Our Father who art in heaven, send to all your Angel of Peace; to humanity the Angel of work."*

It seems that never before has the need been greater for humans to learn how to live in peace.

Peace with their own kind and peace with the environment. Certain times in history there were signs that inspired teachers and enlightened groups have taught a way to creating a better world but examples were soon forgotten, teachings were changed and questions remained unanswered. We are searching back through the centuries to re-connect with original meanings of hidden messages and in this technology and science has come to our aid. Archaeology has uncovered the remains at Qumran giving us an insight into the daily life of the community. Discovery of the Dead Sea Scrolls has given us a clearer view of the way in which the community was organized. These are valuable tools for looking into the past but we must keep in mind that archaeology admits having to use educated guess work at times and even the evidence from the Scrolls needs careful evaluation.

At this point it was important to go into that silent inner space and meditate on Light and Love. Visualize a lighthouse. It is built on solid rock. The sea is turbulent and the storm is wild. See the light beaming in the dark and notice the ship in the distance. Feel the relief of those on the ship as the light guides them to a safe haven. Ask that the light of understanding and tolerance bring Peace to the world.

We all have times when we feel the answers cannot be found to problems we face. Ask for help and inner guidance and allow time for intuition to throw light on the path.

With renewed insight we realize that the Essenes attached great importance to the laws of purity. This is indicated by the specific Rules and also the number of copies found. From the Rules we can have an idea of the way the community was conducted. It gives us a picture of an exclusive organization ruled in an autocratic manner, which insisted on extreme puritanical laws and harsh punishment for even minor transgressions. It also has a totally uncompromising attitude to all 'who walk in the Darkness' and who are therefore 'outsiders.' Not an easy picture to accept for anyone who has a very different image of the Essenes. Discovery of the Scrolls helped to correct the somewhat biased picture presented in earlier descriptions by contemporary and later authors but presented even more questions.

How to reconcile the extreme harshness and intolerance on one hand with an example of a life lived according to the highest ideals? When viewed in this light how do we understand the Essenes? Taking the question even further. What about Jesus, his teaching? Is there any room for that in a Community with Rules such as these? And how is it that an organization with ideas so far ahead of time, a community so disciplined, its members so dedicated could vanish after the destruction of Qumran by the Roman army in AD 68?

Very gradually the answers started to appear. This is can happen when you take a problem into that inner space and call for help to the highest within. A sentence presented itself. *"The view is different depending on where you stand."* The Essene leaders were passionate about guarding the Law, utterly focused on keeping the traditions intact, regarding themselves responsible for the survival of what they believed to be the True Israel. They were the ones who decided on what was to be written in the rules. Their views are mirrored in the War Scroll, the Temple Scroll which point to the ways things would have to be done when the ideal world was established after the victory of Light over the forces of Dark. These were rules for the future. There were Rules which governed the present. Those were for the strictly ascetic communities like Qumran and were far more demanding than the Rules for those Essenes living in villages and towns, as part of the wider community. 'Silent majority?' Was that another flash of insight? Following on that thought it seemed very likely that this silent majority would have left very little written evidence of their views, their innermost beliefs. Could it be that there were many streams of thought, many views and different ways within what we have termed the Essene teaching? Could it be that such changes were slowly taking place over a period of time?

We ask the powers of Light to create a lighthouse within us to show us the way.

**Tuesday Evening**     Angel of Power

Stars

Superior Acts

*"Angel of Power, descend upon my acting body, and direct all my acts."*

Think of the universe. The vast numbers of stars. Science now tells us that we are constantly 'bombarded' by rays from the cosmos. The ancients knew this and their secret symbols taught the initiates how to use these energies. Visualize the great, shining star of Christ love. Open to the power of its rays. Ask that you may be used and so transformed by this love that it becomes mirrored in all your actions. Feel the warmth flooding into your mind, and heart, and know that through this you can reach out to all corners of the world.

"From the point of light within the mind of God let light stream forth into the minds of men. Let light descend on earth. From the point of love within the heart of God let love stream forth into the hearts of men. *May we recognise the Christ within. He has never left us – but we have turned away and forgotten His presence."*

As I view the past hours I realize that often my actions fell short of my intentions. Looking dispassionately, uncritically, I realize that I will only find peace when I let my High Self, the Christ within, take over completely. The still small voice said: *"You will never be alone. Christ is always with you."*

*"Let Light and Love and Power restore the plan on earth."*

## Wednesday Morning

Angel of Sun
Sunrise
Fire of Life
Heart

*"Angel of Sun, enter my Solar Centre and give the fire of life to my whole body."*

Watch the sun rise, or visualize it. Think about its life giving power. The world around you is bathed in light and colour. You feel the warmth on your skin. The birds started singing as dawn came; let your soul sing in response. Sunlight glitters on the dewdrops turning them into a thousand crystals.

Now find the centre within you that glows with the fire of warmth and life and let the rays of the sun enter and renew its power. Without the sun there would be no life. Say again the words of the communion with the Angel of Sun *"...enter my solar centre and give the fire of life to my whole body."* Let it enter and radiate throughout your body touching it, bathing it, healing it. Take a deep breath and feel the sun and air revitalise your whole system. Become receptive of the solar energies, consciously thinking of them, welcoming their help. You are recharging inner batteries.

*"Angel of Sun!*
*There is no warmth without thee,*
*No fire without thee,*
*No life without thee.*
*The green leaves of the trees*

*Do worship thee,*
*And through thee is the tiny wheat kernel*
*Become a river of golden grass*
*Moving with the wind.*
*Through thee is opened the flower*
*In the centre of my body.*
*Therefore will I never hide myself*
*From thee,*
*Angel of Sun,*
*Holy messenger of the Earthly Mother,*
*Enter the holy temple within me*
*And give me the fire of life."*

Now as the symbols and words of these ancient prayers create a powerful resonance within you, let your thoughts dwell on the 'creative love' and speak to the Divine within you. "I don't know you as well as I would like to, but I know and feel the life giving rays of the sun. I feel loved and revitalised by you, by knowing your Life Force, Christ force in me. It fills me with loving-kindness. It is unconditional, eternal love." In silence let the sun warm you and feel peace within you.

Now radiate this life force, this love, symbolised by the sun. Let it fill you and shine through you. Send it out in healing rays to all around you.

*"Be, then, as the sun at noonday*
*Which shineth with light and warmth on all men,*
*And giveth freely and abundantly of her golden glory.*
*Then shall the Fountain of Light flow back to thee,*
*As the sun is never without light*

*For it floweth freely without restraint.*

*.....*

*I bless the Glory and Light...."*


## Wednesday Noon   Peace with the Family

*"Our Father who art in Heaven, send to all your Angel of Peace: to our family and friends the Angel of Love."*

I would like to share with you the unforgettable experience of a walk along the river Ganges at Rishikesh in India. The sound of temple bells carried across the water in the early morning. The sun was still behind the mountains but the sky was luminous and the water shone with the reflection. Kingfishers of all sorts were astir on the river bank. Two small children joined me and we shared an orange. The Wednesday morning meditation in that very special place was one I shall never forget. Love and peace and the whole world became one.

Later on we drove along a high mountain road. The snowcapped Himalayas shone in the distance. We looked down upon eagles cruising in the valleys below us. The road was very narrow and normally I am scared of heights. Our usually confident Sikh driver got out, inspected the next hairpin bend and prayed before negotiating it. At noon we were still driving along the ridge. By then I was well above the world in more ways than one! Fear left and instead came a wonderful certainty of being protected. The morning meditation on the sun merged into the noon contemplation peace with the family and a knowledge that we are all interconnected. The family of mankind. As we neared our noon resting place we met villagers along the road: an old man like a gnarled weather-beaten tree, and a small child. *"Peace with the Family"*, all the world felt like my family. We can if we let the Christ light glow within us feel this love towards all. *Namaste* – the greeting which means *"the spirit in me greets the spirit in you."* Even those who displease you, annoy you or hurt you, do you a service – by providing you with an opportunity for a lesson to love. At some level we are all one. This is what is meant by being one in Christ.

The subject of the noon contemplation is harmony within the close unit of the family.

I think today we have evolved and the family is the whole of mankind. The feeling body expresses itself in its purest form in love. Your loving joins Christ's love. It is what the world needs. Start now. Start with everyone you meet. Every emotion you have sets up a vibration in the feeling body of the planet. Hate and disharmony affect our whole body, and vitality is lessened. Love and harmony give you health and save the world from destruction. This is a law. But it is possible to evolve from that point and so fill the feeling body with love that it shows in all actions. Deviation from this law causes so much suffering. Understanding this law and working in harmony with it can and will change our lives and the world around us.

Send out loving thoughts to the whole family of man. Visualize this world at peace, create it, and know that it will become reality.

*"Dawn at Rishikesh"*

## Wednesday Evening

Angel of Love
Superior Feelings and Emotions
Cosmic Ocean of Love

*"Angel of Love, descend upon my Feeling Body and purify my feelings."*

It is thought that the Essenes were in touch with the eastern mystical teachings and their great cultural traditions. Divisions are man made. Love is universal and 'stronger than the currents of deep waters'.

In this meditation we first develop love towards ourselves. Some people find this very difficult – for others it poses no problem. But until you can accept yourself it is difficult to love others selflessly. Think of your body: this wonderful fascinating, intricate, engineering feat evolved over thousands, millions of years. And the mind! What a marvelous instrument, created by the Master craftsman. Speak to yourself with love and encouragement, appreciating the unique divine spark within you.

The second stage is to think of a friend. Someone more or less the same age, and still on this plane of existence, someone still alive. This is the easiest as it is not difficult to let feeling of warmth well up towards someone who is near and dear to us.

Next take the image of a person whom you neither particularly like or dislike. Don't just think of feeling love, but let it actually well up in you as a warm, glowing feeling. Again, some people find they can call forth such emotion easier than others. Temperament has a large part to play here. But keep trying, don't give up at the first difficulty.

The fourth stage is perhaps the most difficult – but what a breakthrough when we finally get it to work! Visualize a person whom you dislike. Someone who may have been unkind to you or even harmed you. And bring the same feeling of love towards this person. It is possible. Somewhere deep within, possibly buried under many layers, is the Divine Spark waiting to be liberated by love. *"The spirit in me greets the spirit in you."* We line up these four, visualize them and direct the same love towards all of them. This is the preparation.

In the fifth stage we go a step further and we direct the same feeling of love towards all around us in an ever-increasing circle: our group, or family, the community in which we live, the locality, our country, our part of the world. We forget ourselves and let our love flow in an ever larger circle encompassing the whole world, reaching out to all forms of life, animate and inanimate, seen and unseen. We hold ourself still in this ocean of cosmic love. "Love is stronger than the currents of deep waters. Love is stronger than death."

## Thursday Morning   Angel of Water
Rivers, Sea, Blood, Circulation

*"Angel of Water, enter my blood and give the water of life to*
*my whole body."*

What wonder, what miraculous thing is water. Perhaps only the desert dweller or traveller can appreciate it fully. Visualize the rain falling on parched soil. See the miracle of new growth which comes when the water has touched the seed. Hear, with your inner ears, the waves breaking on the seashore in a steady rhythmic sound. Hear the sound of a brook splashing, spilling over rocks. Listen, see, smell and taste, using your subtler senses. Become still like the surface of a quiet mountain lake.

*"Let my love flow towards thee, Heavenly Father,*
*As the river flows to the sea.*
*And let thy love flow to me, Heavenly Father*
*As the gentle rain doth kiss the earth."*

Visualize a fountain. With each breath you draw in feel the life-giving water enter and fill you, rising higher until it surges up through the crown into the sunlight. There it turns into thousands of shimmering golden drops of water cascading down over you, showering you with the love of Christ. Let this holy, life-giving water enter you, fill your blood, and circulate through you.

*"In my blood flow a thousand pure springs,*
*And vapours, and clouds, and all the waters*
*That spread over all the seven kingdoms....*
*Angel of Water,*

*Holy messenger of the Earthly Mother,*
*Enter the blood that flows through me,*
*Wash my body in the rain*
*That falls from heaven*
*And give me the Water of Life.......*
*Heavenly Father, and Thou, Angel of Water,*
*We are thankful to thee, and we bless thy name.*
*A flood of love welleth up*
*From the hidden places beneath the Earth:*
*For the Brotherhood is blessed forever*
*In the Holy Waters of Life."*


## Thursday Noon    Peace with the Mind

*"Our Father who art in Heaven, send to all your Angel of Peace; to our*
*mind the Angel of Power."*

Thought is Power! It can create in accordance with the Law, or it can be destructive if it is not in harmony with it. The decision is ours. The important thing is to remember that our thoughts are powerful, valuable tools, and to be used as such.

According to the ancient teaching we have an individual thinking body formed by our thoughts. If these thoughts are creative, loving and positive, that is in harmony with the Law, then this thinking body will be healthy, and so will our physical body. The root cause of disharmony or disease in the body is very often due to wrong thinking.

The planetary thinking body is made up of thoughts of all individuals all over the world. If we allow negative thoughts to fill our mind then these will attract other dark and fearful thoughts. But loving positive thoughts are contagious too! We must feed our thinking body with the right kind of food: positive, loving thoughts. Over-emphasis on the negative, destructive thoughts gives them more importance, greater substance. Our individual efforts link with the cosmic Body of Thought. We can join our thoughts with the thoughts that are creative and loving. You may feel unable to do much to help the world. But this is not so. Your loving thoughts are very powerful.

**Thursday Evening**    Angel of Wisdom
                        Superior thoughts
                        Thinking Body


*"Angel of Wisdom, descend upon my Thinking Body and enlighten*
*all my thoughts."*


As we follow the routine of weekly meditation over a course of time our thoughts and ideas change gradually. It is not so much the number of minutes which can be set apart but the intention and the frequency of the flashbacks from the material to the spiritual which brings about the transformation. The morning meditations create a new harmony between earthly forces and our body. The unseen is becoming real! At noon a few minutes on the aspect of the Sevenfold Peace and a quick thought at how I can put it into practice in my life; how to love, to heal and help. Then, before going to sleep, I let my thoughts become attuned to the Highest. It is said that the Polynesian healer priests, the Kahunas, used powerful imagery in forming their prayers. The water rising in a well was likened to creative thoughts rising inside you. The water or rain pouring down and filling the cup to the brim was the request granted. They also instructed those who came to them for healing to visualize, in detail, the desired condition and called this 'making a thought form cluster' like a bunch of grapes or cluster of seeds. Wrong intentions, blockages due to disharmony, and doubts are the three major obstacles to effective prayer. Remove these and your prayer will re-mould your life, your world. If the conscious mind says it is impossible for the world to be saved from destroying itself then the unconscious mind will follow suit. Guard and guide your thoughts, therefore aim high! *"You must be afraid of nothing. Be willing to do the most unusual things without hesitation. Always remember that you are functioning from a spiritual, not from a human level of consciousness. You are working with My laws."* (Eileen Caddy, "Footprints on the Path.")

We link in thought with all others praying for the world. We link also with the higher realms. Each time a negative thought comes into your mind counteract it with a positive one, and use this to guide your feelings, and all your actions. By doing this we join the heavenly powers in creating a new world.

*"Thou hast made known unto me*
*The deep, mysterious things,*
*All things exist by Thee and there is none beside Thee;*
*By Thy Law*
*Thou hast directed my heart*
*That I set my steps straight forward*
*Upon the right paths*
*And walk where Thy presence is."*

**Friday Morning**     Angel of Air

Air, Lungs


*"Angel of Air, enter my lungs and give the air of life to
my whole body."*


As I wake up I hear the wind in the trees, the energy of the Angel
of Air. The lungs look like an inverted tree. Directing the attention of
the air flowing in, cleaning and invigorating the whole body, think of
your lungs in wonder and admiration. What an amazing mechanism.
Draw in the life-giving air, the vital force, the 'prana'.

*"In the midst of the fresh air of the forest, there shall thou find the
Angel of Air. Patiently she waits for thee to quit the dark and crowded
holes of the city. Seek her there and drink deeply of the healing draught
which she doth offer thee. Breathe long and deeply, that the Angel of Air
may be brought within thee. For the rhythm of thy breath is the key of
knowledge which doth reveal the Holy Law."*


Watch the breath go in – and out – gently, without effort.
Mindfulness of breathing is an exercise used widely in many forms
of meditation. Think of the energy flooding in with every breath. Let
all the cares, worries, and impurities go: flow away with every out-
breath. Never force it – just let the air come and go rhythmically until
you can envisage yourself full of this wonderful life-giving air of
vital energy.

*"For, lo, the eternal and sovereign luminous space, where rule the
unnumbered stars, is the air we breathe in and the air we breathe out."*

Hold the breath for a few seconds at the point between breathing in and breathing out. Let a second or two elapse at the end of your exhaling before drawing in breath but do not labour at this – just enjoy it. It seems that the mind is most receptive to knowledge when natural rhythm is followed during the learning process and information is best absorbed at the point when the breath changes from the in breath to the out breath.

*"And in the moment between the breathing in and the breathing out are hidden all the mysteries of the Infinite Garden. Angel of Air, Holy messenger of the Earthly Mother, enter deep within me, as the swallow plummets from the sky, that I may know the secrets of the wind and the music of the stars"*

Remain in this stillness.

I breathe in God: and send out light and love. Let each breath do this now… And let it continue to do this throughout the day, while you are busty at your tasks.

# Friday Noon    Peace with the Body

*"Our Father who art in Heaven, send to all your Angel of Peace, to our body the Angel of Life."*

Even with today's scientific knowledge, the body retains some of its mysteries. How miraculous the functioning of the cells, the organs, the bones. Look upon it with admiration, appreciation and affection. Care for it like you would look after a valuable instrument, because this is what it is, a tool with which to create a garden on earth.

*"The body and the heart and the mind are a chariot, a horse, and a driver. The chariot is the body, forged in strength to do the will of the Heavenly Father and the Earthly Mother. The heart is the fiery steed, glorious and courageous who carries the chariot bravely, whether the road be smooth or whether stones and fallen trees lie in its path. And the driver is the mind, holding the reins of wisdom, seeing from above what lieth on the far horizon, charting the course of hoof and wheels."* (Plato - rephrased)

At this point in evolution we must find harmony between mind, body and spirit. *"To think with the heart and not with the mind alone"* is our task. In the early days of the race primitive instincts and emotions ruled. The recent ages have seen tremendous developments of the rational mind. Now it is time for the spirit to be dominant. Those who know this may be in the minority just yet, but their numbers are growing: they are Essenes of today, the preparers of the way. By being in harmony with our surroundings and environment and in peace with ourselves and our fellowmen, we create conditions in which the body can be wholly healthy – whole; holy; healthy. *"Give us today our daily bread."* The right food for the mind, body and spirit is what will help build a new generation and a new world.

# CONCLUSION

When the similarities between Essenes and early Christian groups became obvious from the Scrolls there were some anxious voices raised. Here were manuscripts predating Christianity which showed sayings, beliefs and practices which we had been taught to regard as unique to Christianity. As we learnt more about the Essenes we gained  wider knowledge about the Jewish background from which Christianity arose,  The similarities between the two groups also made for greater understanding of early Christianity.

The Scrolls and the early Christian documents discovered in 1945 at Nag Hammadi in Upper Egypt showed the great diversity of religious groups at that time in Palestine. Later on many of these beliefs came to be considered heresies and their voices  silenced by the official Church which by then had lost contact with its Jewish routes and was now the state religion.

There is no mention of the name Essene in the New Testament and other Christina writings. Neither do we find the name in the Scrolls as the group referred to themselves as 'children of the light' and other such designations. At that time in Jewish history the Essenes occupied the leading role as teachers of the esoteric tradition. Guardians of the ancient wisdom they were bound by oath of secrecy. Perhaps it is not surprising that they appeared to have vanished after the destruction of Qumram in AD 68 and the national calamity in the years that followed.

We are lucky to live at a time when so much new information is coming to light and when we are allowed to ask questions without having to fear persecution. A wider knowledge of the Essenes and their beliefs will help us to understand early Christianity better.

A new portrait of Jesus of Nazareth can now be seen against the background of 1st Century Galilean life and thought. His message is of the Kingdom of God to be found in your heart. It is the potential in all of us. I use the term "Christ" not as a name but   to describe the principle of the divine power of unlimited, infinite love.

Let us become a point of light to radiate love and peace to the world.

# BOOKS RECOMMENDED FOR FURTHER STUDY

Vermes, Géza
The Complete Dead Sea Scrolls in English
Penguin Books - London 1997

*This is the best English translation of the Dead Sea Scrolls.*

Vermes, Géza
Jesus and the World of Judaism
Fortress Press – Minneapolis 1983

*This book contains much valuable information about the Essene and their times*

Edmond Bordeaux Szekely
The Gospel of the Essenes – The Unknown Books of The Essenes
& Lost Scrolls of The Essene  Brotherhood

Translated and edited from the original Hebrew and Aramaic by
Edmond Bordeaux Szekely

*In the Preface to the 1974 edition of the Gospel of the Essenes, Szekely wrote: "It was not easy to be faithful to the original, and to present the eternal truths in a way that would appeal to 20th Century man."*

*Unfortunately it has not been possible to locate the manuscripts from which some of the above translations have been made but Szekely's  inspired interpretation has given our age new ways of living in harmony with the world around us.*

I have tried to find suitable terms for that within us which has been called by many names: the High Self, the Divine, the Spirit Within and have used the term 'Christ within.' The meditations in this book should serve as an inspiration rather than a guide to be copied. They are records of personal inner journeys shared with the reader. As each individual follows his or her path so the meditations change from week to week to suit the need or the occasion.

Use the table on the next page as a guideline which may be referred to frequently until the daily and weekly pattern of communication with the Heavenly and Earthly Kingdoms has become imprinted on the memory.

# DAILY MEDITATIONS

## Morning Communions with the Forces of the Visible Realms

| Saturday | Sunday | Monday | Tuesday | Wednesday | Thursday | Friday |
|---|---|---|---|---|---|---|
| **MOTHER EARTH** | **EARTH** | **LIFE** | **JOY** | **SUN** | **WATER** | **AIR** |
| Food from Mother Earth | Topsoil / Growth of New Life | Trees / Vitality | Beauty and Harmony | Sunrise | Rivers, sea | Breath of Life |
| Digestive System | Regeneration glands | Bone Structure Muscles | The Effect of Positive Thoughts on the Nervous System | Heart Solar Centre | Blood Circulation | Lungs Breath |

## The Noon Meditaton THE SEVENFOLD PEACE

| Saturday | Sunday | Monday | Tuesday | Wednesday | Thursday | Friday |
|---|---|---|---|---|---|---|
| Kingdom of the Heavenly Father | Kingdom of the Earthly Mother | Culture | Humanity (Social Peace) | Family (Feeling, Body) | Mind (Thinking Body) | Body (Acting Body) |

## Evening Communions with the Powers of the Invisible Realms

| Saturday | Sunday | Monday | Tuesday | Wednesday | Thursday | Friday |
|---|---|---|---|---|---|---|
| **ETERNAL LIFE** | **CREATIVE WORK** | **PEACE** | **POWER** | **LOVE** | **WISDOM** | **THE HEAVENLY FATHER AND I ARE ONE** |
| Planets | Bees | Crescent Moon | Stars | Superior Feelings | Superior Thoughts | |
| Overcoming Gravity | Creative Work of Man | Peace within | Power of Superior Acts (of good) | Unconditional Love | | |
| "Lift up your hearts!" | We are co-creators with God | "My peace I give unto you." | Cosmic Ocean of Life | Cosmic Ocean of Love | Cosmic Currents | Union with the Cosmic Ocean of Divinity |

# THE ESSENE NETWORK INTERNATIONAL

Founded in 1987 to popularise closer co-operation with Angels through the use of daily meditations, the Essene Network now seeks ways to help people adjust to new spiritual energies and changing consciousness. We are all becoming aware of the great 'Awakening' of our Earth and are caught up in the process of becoming divine. We desperately need to seek ways to ground the cosmic energies of love and light for the sake of our earth and all humankind.

We hold to the ideas of commitment to the Daily Meditation, working with the Angels, a belief in reincarnation and through vegetarianism, a special regard for the Life Force in foods. We hold regular gatherings and retreats to spread the knowledge of the Essene Teachings and to provide the chance for people of like minds to come together in an easy, loving and joyful atmosphere. Some of our members also run Angel workshops, retreats and weekends.

## MEMBERSHIP BENEFITS

* Quarterly newsletter        * Free book on joining
* News on other allied events     * Distant healing
* Members discounts on workshops, retreats and other events

For more information visit:

## WWW.ESSENENETWORK.ORG